TO HELL AND BACK

TO HELL AND BACK

A TRUE TALE OF HEROISM IN WORLD WAR ONE

NEVILLE BARLEY

HISTORY INTO PRINT

First published by
History into Print, 56 Alcester Road,
Studley, Warwickshire, B80 7LG in 2010

www.history-into-print.com

ISBN: 978-1-85858-337-2

A Cataloguing in Publication Record
for this title is available from the British Library.

Typeset in Baskerville
Printed in Great Britain by
Hobbs the Printers Ltd.

CONTENTS

PREFACE

Wilfrid Barley was born in September 1894, the seventh child and second son of Richard and Emma Barley. The family business in the Worcestershire village of Inkberrow was general builders and undertakers. On leaving school at the age of 14 years, he was apprenticed to the undertaking side of the business, but when the First World War was declared he was busy learning painting and decorating.

He died in late 1974, but it was many years later before the family, while clearing out drawers, discovered a note pad under paper lining at the bottom of the drawer. It was a diary that he had kept throughout the First World War. He had never mentioned it, and not even his wife knew of its existence. The original diary is in the 1914-1918 archives at Sunderland Polytechnic. This is the story of Wilfrid's war, based entirely on the record he kept so meticulously. This is his story – a voice from the grave.

WILFRID BARLEY aged 20 years.

Chapter One

BEFORE THE FIGHTING

On September 2nd 1914, just a few days before his 20th birthday, Wilfrid set out with 12 other young men from the then small village of Inkberrow to '*do our duty*' by enlisting in the Royal Worcesters where he served in the 1st, 4th and 5th Battalions. Little did they realise on that morning when Wilfrid assured his mother that he would be home by Christmas, how few of them were ever to return and what grievous injuries would be inflicted on some of those who, like Wilfrid, were lucky enough to come home. He told his mother that he would be home by Christmas, but '*I could tell from the look on her face that she did not believe me.*'

After medical examination the little party from Inkberrow moved to Worcester Norton barracks where overcrowding was so bad that most of them were forced to sleep in the open air. One blanket each was all that was provided but they were given a couple of footballs so that on the really cold nights they could get up and have a kick around! Diet consisted of '*bread and marmalade for breakfast, stew and more stew for lunch* (main meal) *and bread and margarine for tea*'. An enterprising baker would appear at teatime and most of the lads' money would be spent on such little luxuries as cakes.

After about 5 days Wilfrid was moved to Torpoint near Plymouth where the men were housed in tents and given two blankets. Unfortunately the tents were not fit for purpose and some blew away in the autumn gales that were all too frequent in that part of the world. It was here that training for fighting started. The first hour from 6.30 - 7.30a.m. was taken up with physical exercises and this was followed by breakfast of bread and a small piece of bacon. Days were filled with bayonet practice and musketry (rifle) training with 20-mile route marches on two days a week.

It was during his time at Torpoint that Wilfrid was fortunate to be invited to the home of a retired naval officer. He, his wife and two daughters, entertained some of the men, making sure that they had the occasional square meal.

Still wearing their civilian clothes, it was not long before the recruits were moved to Tregantle Fort, about 8 miles from Torpoint. There was no room in the fort and previously ordered accommodation huts failed to materialise, so they were housed in tents which were pitched on sloping ground and their days were spent in endless drilling exercises. Only once a week were they allowed to leave camp and the three shillings and sixpence (17½p) per week pay did not go far for beer, cigarettes and other extras. By now Wilfrid's civilian clothes were threadbare and worn out as the soldiers had been forced to wear them day and night. The officers were ashamed for the men 'to go out of camp looking like tramps,' so it was that while at the Fort they were issued with blue suits.

One Sunday morning, after Church Parade, the men were lined up and told by the adjutant that they were soon to be going to the front line; however, they were not to be afraid as the Germans shot into the air. Each man was expected to *'kill ten of the devils before you get killed.'* (Very reassuring!)

For the next two months the Section was moved to Raglan Barracks in Devonport. Here they had a bed a pillow and tables with cutlery – the height of luxury. They were now allowed out of barracks several times a week and Wilfrid was able to visit previously made friends. During his stay he had the temerity to ask the Company Sergeant Major for leave. This was refused but he, ever resourceful, asked to see the Commanding Officer who granted him four days: one day to get home, two days at home and one to return. It was the lull before the storm as it was not long after this that he was drafted to France with the 1st Battalion of the Royal Worcestershire Regiment. Each Battalion consisted of one thousand men, divided into four Companies and each Company was divided into four platoons. A Sergeant led each platoon that was then divided into Sections of 15 soldiers, each led by a Corporal.

On Wednesday March 24th 1915 three hundred men, including some NCOs and three officers, marched off to Devonport train station to the accompaniment of the Regimental Band. As they marched through Devonport they were cheered all the way by local people. They were given a jolly good send off in spite of the early hour for they arrived at the station at 7.00a.m. At 8.00a.m. the train left for Southampton, arriving there at 12 noon. It was not until 8.00p.m. that they boarded the ship that took them to Le Havre, arriving at 3.00a.m. the next day.

Chapter Two

WELCOME TO FRANCE

The welcome the Tommies (infantry soldiers) received in France was outstanding. Whenever the men were marching large crowds cheered them on their way. It was noticeable that, in France, only women were working in the fields. They worked really hard and were out from daybreak to sunset. There was much less machinery than in England and it seemed that most of the men had been conscripted into the army. Most of the British soldiers were unable to speak French but the Section had several interpreters. However, *'The French lassies were always ready to give us a few lessons!'* Another difference between France and England was that conscientious objection to serving in the Forces was not allowed so all males of the right age, whatever their social standing, had no option but to serve. (Liberté, Egalité, Fraternité).

There followed a 5-mile march to the Base Camp where the Tommies were packed like sardines into tents. However, the weather was good and all were in high spirits and looking forward to entering the theatre of conflict for which they had been trained. On the following day, in the afternoon, the Section marched back to Le Havre and boarded a train for Estaires, which was about 12 miles behind the front line, arriving at 4p.m. on Saturday March 27th.

Chapter Three

IN THE TRENCHES

Having arrived in Estaires, they began the 12 miles march to the front line trenches. In the distance it was possible to see star (illumination) shells exploding, giving the appearance of a firework display. Much louder explosions that were caused by powerful shells landing on the ground not too far away occasionally punctuated these star shell bursts. *'They were Fritz's* (German) *shells'* and the men soon learnt that their first taste of the trenches would be ditches on the side of the road as they dived for cover. Soon these shells were bursting within three hundred yards of the intrepid marchers, spraying shrapnel over a wide area. It was pitch dark and the only light provided was from the star shells. The march could better be described as a stumble as it included many falls into bomb craters and dives for the ditches. This was the soldiers' first introduction to war.

It was 10p.m., and dark, when the soldiers arrived at the 60ft. Headquarters dugout where the Commander, deputy Commander, Adjutant and *'a few more spare Officers with plenty of staff to wait on them'* were housed, safe and behind the front line. It was from here that the signallers relayed messages to the front line Commanders. They were tired and glad to have arrived. Each man was assigned to a Company,

Wilfrid's being 'A' Company. There, he reported to the Sergeant Major who ordered his Company to stand by for a charge but thankfully this never materialised - perhaps the Sergeant Major was just testing their mettle. They were all pretty weary and so they were excused duties that night and were able to get some well-earned rest. They were split into small groups and each group was assigned to a small dugout but with rifles and bayonets at the ready. This arrangement ensured that if a German shell landed a direct hit on one dugout, only a small number of men would be killed.

Cross Section of a Front Line Trench

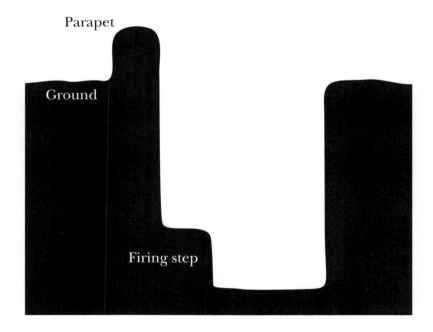

The soldiers, equipped with loaded rifles and bayonets, proceeded along the communication trench to the front line trenches that were arranged in a zigzag pattern. At this time, men were expected to shave, polish their buttons and salute an officer while in the trenches. The weather was good and the trenches were surprisingly clean, tidy and well-ordered. The high parapet meant that even Wilfrid, who was 6ft. 1inch tall, could walk along the trench standing upright without being seen by the enemy. Unfortunately if any man was foolish enough to put his head above the parapet in daylight, he was soon despatched by a German sniper. At the front of the trench was a fire step onto which the fighters could stand to fire their rifles and so repel any attack. Reserve ammunition was neatly arranged along the front of the trench ready for immediate use.

Chapter Four

SOLDIERS AT 'THE READY'

Most of the shells from the German guns were landing behind the line of the forward trenches and there was little grenade throwing at this time. It was a time of stalemate with neither side gaining ground. At night, each Platoon posted two men on lookout, taking it in turns to stand for an hour and sit for an hour. Any man who fell asleep on his watch, either standing or sitting, was shot. The most likely time for an attack to be launched by the enemy was dusk or dawn and at these times the whole platoon would be standing at the ready. During the rest of the day there were always two sentries from each Platoon on duty, and the other men spent time cleaning rifles and clearing up the trench. The men were allowed to light fires in the trenches as long as they did not produce enough smoke to give away their position and invite a few trench mortars from the Germans. *(Tommy must have his cup of tea!)*

For the first six months rations were good - bread, butter, jam, biscuits, bully beef (corned beef) and potatoes, all being brought up to the front line trenches where each man cooked his own food. Gas masks were always ready and each sentry had an empty shell case to

use as a gong in the event of a gas attack. Food parcels and letters from home were brought up to the front line trenches and *'a smiling man is a man who has plenty of letters and parcels from home'*. In the good weather aircraft would be flying overhead on either reconnaissance missions or involved in dogfights.

Sopwith Camel

After every three to six-day stint in the trenches the Sherwood Foresters relieved Wilfrid's Platoon. The men then marched back to their billet that, at this time, was a farmhouse twelve miles behind the front line trenches. What bliss to be able to take boots off weary feet, dry any wet clothing and have a proper wash down, all this followed by a good night's sleep on straw palliasses! Unfortunately for him, at 8a.m. on the next day, Wilfrid was ordered, together with three of his comrades, to march back to the trenches (a three-hour trek), do three hours trench digging followed by the three-hour march back. This was repeated, with different parties of 4 men, on each of the 3-6 days spent back at the billet. On other days they were free to walk back to any nearby villages where an estaminet, (small pub, and café) and Y.M.C.A. canteens had everything on sale *'except our discharge!'* Most of the soldiers' meagre wage was spent in the local estaminet or épicerie. The owners of the estaminet were willing to set up quite near the front line and occasionally in the communication trenches.

During this period of the war, a captured German soldier said he was amazed to see that none of the Tommies were equipped with machine guns as this was so on the German side. *'We were our own machine gun, firing 15 rounds a minute.'* It was also during this period that the owner of an estaminet in a communication trench was discovered to be a German spy. He was duly bayoneted.

On the morning of 19th April, Wilfrid was selected to train in grenade warfare in what was known as the Suicide Club. Here he was taught to make his own 'jam-pot' bombs (home-made grenades). He was also given a psychological indoctrination in the importance of *'being British,'* and how they were all expected to do their duty. During this training they were inspected by Sir John French (The memorial plaque in his memory is in St George's Church, Ypres, or 'Ieper', as it is now known). The training was finished by May 6th and Wilfrid realised an attack on the German defences must be imminent.

Chapter Five

ATTACK!

On the evening of May 7th large, numbers of soldiers were assembled ready for the attack which was to take place the following morning. It was to be in several waves with the Worcesters in the third wave. By 4.00a.m. on the 8th everyone was in place. It began with an hour's bombardment from the heavy artillery followed by a push from the Infantry. At 6a.m. Wilfrid's Division, equipped with rifle, bayonet, ammunition and bombs, was ready for this. The soldiers were paid twice a month and always tried to spend their money before going into battle, in case they did not return.

During the first two waves of the onslaught 20,000 men were lost. It was difficult for the third wave to push forward because of the large numbers of walking, stumbling and wounded struggling to get back

behind their lines; also large numbers of dead and dying British soldiers were lying in no-man's land, (the area between the British and German lines). Men were being blown high in the air by German fire, and trench mortars had almost destroyed the trenches which, the day before, had been all ship-shape and in order. The moans and groans of the dying were punctuated by the rat-tat-tat of rifle fire with many men lying with arms and legs blown off. However much pity welled up in the hearts of those still standing, they were forbidden to stop and help their comrades. Thirty-five soldiers, including Wilfrid, who had been trained to throw the 'jam-jar' bombs, received the order to get within 36ft. of the German trenches to lob their home made bombs into the enemy trenches. Only six returned.

After he returned to his trench, Wilfrid walked a short way down to his post, counting 70 men lying dead and wounded. He was given permission to rest for one hour and spent the time walking down the trench, giving water from his bottle to the wounded. Although the Germans continued a heavy bombardment, most of the injured and dead from the front line trenches were, during the night, taken down the communication trench to the headquarters dugout for evacuation or burial the following day. The Germans counter-attacked the next day and adopted the tactic of stripping the uniforms from the dead Tommies in no man's land, changing into them and hoping to deceive the British. The tactic did not work because *'we bombed them away,'* and all the Germans who came near enough to the British trenches to throw their grenades were killed. For the next three days sporadic skirmishing continued with neither side gaining any ground.

The Division held their trench until 12th May and was then relieved and able to return, at midnight, to their billet where a field kitchen and cooks were waiting with a good square meal. Tea, rum and food were available and this was the first food and first drink, other than water, that they had been given for four days. At the billet they found 300 soldiers waiting to bring their company up to strength again. When the roll call took place it was found that the Brigade had lost 450 men. Wilfrid had survived his first experience of war *'with just a few scratches'* but it was more difficult to eradicate the mental scars, having witnessed and experienced what no 20 year-old would expect to see or go through. During this time the weather was quite stormy and conditions in the trenches were unpleasant.

Chapter Six

BACK TO SCHOOL

On May 17th Wilfrid was ordered back to the bomb training school in Estaires but *'when I arrived I found very few of the old faces left'*. Training in grenade warfare continued until June 7th and life in Estaires was pretty good compared with life in the trenches. Concerts were put on for the forces and the men played football when off duty. *'It was very amusing when a German aircraft appeared as everyone had to take cover'*.

It was not all fun and games because after only one day in Estaires there was a Court Martial for two nineteen year-old deserters. One was sentenced to a long prison term but unfortunately the other was shot. This greatly upset Wilfrid. *'I can see his face now as I write these few lines – enough to break his mother's heart'*. That night he dreamt that he was back in Inkberrow in the village pub, The Bull's Head. Here he was giving a lecture on bomb-making and the whole village had turned out to hear it. He woke to find it was only a dream – *'a great disappointment'*.

While in Estaires a German shell landed in his billet and destroyed the sleeping area. Fortunately it happened during the day but even so there were some casualties and he lost all his belongings as they had been left back at the billet.

Chapter Seven

JUNE 10th 1915 – SEPTEMBER 22nd 1915

This period of just over three months takes up almost thirty pages of the diary in which Wilfrid made succinct notes on most days. Much of it is repetitive with three or four days' fighting in the trenches at various points on the front line followed by several days in the billets. This involved a march of several miles to small villages that had often been badly damaged by shells. However some days, and the story they tell, are worthy of special mention.

On June 11th the Company were ordered to the trenches in the new location of Neuve Chapelle where it remained for six days, suffering about 20 casualties in both dead and wounded as a result of German shelling. The weather was wet, and as a result the men found the trenches very wet and dirty. After a few days in billets Wilfrid's Section were in new trenches at Orberis Ridge where on June 29th an 8-inch German shell dropped right beside him, throwing him to the ground, but fortunately for him it failed to explode.

On July 1st the Company were relieved and moved to new billets at Sailly (now Saily Sallisel) and on the next day Wilfrid noted that he had a bath *'which we were all in need of, as we were beginning to get plenty of company!'* This rest period was followed by more time in the trenches where the Section was sent on patrol in no man's land. At this point, the officer in command was taken prisoner by the Germans but all the men escaped. It was also at this time that a party of grass cutters went out (the grass in no man's land having become very long) Unfortunately, all these men were either killed or wounded *by our own machine guns owing to a wrong order being given to the gunner.*

By the 10th July the weather had changed and it was very hot. A German attack was launched but was repulsed, resulting in many casualties on both sides. Later, while back in billets, a British shell landed in the billet killing the Sergeant and wounding a number of others. Moving from the trenches to billets took place regularly until 28th July when they were able to have another bath. The following day was a memorable one for Wilfrid as he was promoted to Lance Corporal and celebrated with a swim in the afternoon.

On August 8th the Battalion moved back to Sailly where, by the river, there was a horse show with jumping and displays of guns and transport wagons. The Divisional Band was in attendance. While here they attended a lecture on gas warfare and gas masks. Wilfrid and seven other soldiers were chosen to walk through a shed full of gas. Following this training they returned to their trenches which were only twenty yards from the German trenches. It was here that a German sniper hit the Company Officer, Mr Smith-Osborne, who died fifteen minutes later.

September 24th was Wilfrid's 21st birthday; He was out trench digging. *'My birthday present from the army!'* At 4.00a.m. the following day the Brigade made a Charge, capturing two lines of German trenches with heavy loss of life on the German side. They were only able to hold the ground gained for a few hours after which the British were pushed back to their original trenches with heavy losses on their side. The soldiers were then ordered to dig new trenches, this time 50 yds. from the German lines.

Chapter Eight

SEPTEMBER 22nd 1915 – FEBRUARY 18th 1916

Following a period in Estaires, the Section marched 10 miles to new billets in Hirkingham. This time they were billeted in a house with some French soldiers with whom Wilfrid got on really well. He also slept on a bed – the first time for a long time – and it resulted in him oversleeping and being late on parade the next day! October 15th saw him in the trenches again in front of Armentières. These trenches were very wet and dirty. On 29th he was sent on another course, this time in trench mortars. He stayed in reserve billets in front of Armentières until Christmas.

Christmas day turned out to be quite enjoyable. The Commanding Officer had ordered two pigs to be sent from England and the men made a feast of pork and plum (Christmas) pudding. There were two barrels of beer and plenty of cigarettes and tobacco. *'Not much like a war being on.'* Unfortunately, it was not to last because on Boxing Day he was ordered back to the trenches where *'we had a rough time with the mud and bullets flying about.'* On 26th January the Section moved to new billets. The following day was the Kaiser's birthday and the British launched a heavy artillery bombardment causing much loss of life on the German side. On February 10th, the Section was moved to trenches in Chapelle Armentières where, on 11th, they were shelled and had their first experience of gas being used. This was to be the prelude to something much more agreeable.

The next day Wilfrid was told he could have home leave. After walking seven miles to Base he marched a further eight miles to the train station, where, at 4.30a.m. on the 13th, he boarded the train for Boulogne. After a rough crossing to Folkestone he took a train for London where he changed to a train for Birmingham, arriving at midnight. From here he hired a car and two hours later he was in his sister's house in Crabbs Cross not far from his home at Inkberrow, arriving at 2.00a.m. Here he was able to have a bath and was given a good breakfast before making his way home to Inkberrow where until 18th *'I had a glorious time, quite a contrast to the trenches.'*

Chapter Nine

FEBRUARY 19th 1916 – JULY 1st 1916

Having enjoyed 5 days at home, Wilfrid started the long journey back to billets. The train took him, via Birmingham, from Redditch to Folkestone where he caught the boat for Boulogne. The first night he slept in a so-called rest camp four miles from Boulogne. It consisted of a canvas tent and only one blanket per soldier for a night that was bitterly cold. He arrived back at his Battalion to find deep snow. On 29th he travelled by train to Bethune from where he marched to billets at Brécey where a British contingent had relieved the French forces. Following an inspection by the Army Corps Commander, and Battalion parades, on 6th March his Section marched the ten miles through very hilly country to new billets. A couple of days later he records that he was repairing and detonating bombs, and on that day they *'fetched a German aeroplane down.'*

A couple of days later, after getting bombs ready, they marched the eight miles to the trenches at Souchez. These trenches were on some very large hills: territory that had been hard won by the French at the cost of one hundred thousand lives. The trenches were anything between ten and a hundred yards from the German lines. The trenches at Souchez had no rest dugouts and the communication trench back to billets in the village was about three miles long. The cellars in the village were full of dead bodies and most of the village had been destroyed. The hills in no man's land were also littered with many bodies, both French and German. Nine soldiers, including Wilfrid, were warned to be ready for bomb throwing and on 11th March two of the nine were killed and two were injured. The next few days saw heavy artillery bombardment from both sides and much activity in the air. Three German aircraft and one British were lost on 14th.

Two days later the group was relieved and ordered to march to Stainet from where they moved to new trenches at Grenay. The next few days were occupied with marches to dig trenches around a nine-mile radius before returning to Grenay. While here they suffered heavy bombardment from the German guns. One trench collapsed and buried a number of men. On April 5th Wilfrid and his colleague, A. Davis, were ordered to rebuild the parapet wall with sandbags and, while on this task, they found two German spies almost in their own trenches. They were listening for information on British troop movements and were quickly despatched with grenades. After this episode they moved to a dugout at Souchez station for a rest period during which heavy German shelling penned them in. The Germans then scored a direct shell strike. Of the thirty-six men in there at the time, three were killed and buried, six were wounded and twelve suffered severe shell shock. Although coming under heavy shell-fire, the survivors managed to get into a trench nearby but, unfortunately, they lost all their equipment, including rifles. It was not until 2a.m. on April 10th that they reached new billets at Bouvigny where, in very warm weather, they were sent trench digging. In mid May the Germans sent gas over followed by an infantry assault which was repulsed.

The war continued with very heavy artillery shelling from both sides, but little infantry activity. Life for Wilfrid revolved round manning front-line trenches followed by time in either the billet or the reserve trenches. The end of the following month saw another move to new trenches, about one hundred yards from the German lines, not far from Souchez.

On June 2nd the Platoon Sergeant was killed, and ten days later Wilfrid and A. Davis were ordered over the top to put out barbed wire. *'We had a narrow escape.'* Unfortunately the Germans located them and opened fire with machine guns but all the bullets missed them. In mid June the Section moved back to Battalion headquarters where there were *'Battalion parades from morning 'til night!'* On June 24th they marched the twelve miles to the station at Lillers and thence by train to Amiens followed by a ten miles march to Saint Souvenir in the Somme district.

Chapter Ten

LIFE ON THE SOMME

On the first full day here, and for the next three days, during which the weather was warm but often wet, the Section underwent further training. On June 30th the Worcesters moved into reserve trenches ready for an offensive which was scheduled for dawn on July 1st.

It started with a heavy bombardment followed by an infantry assault by the front line troops. Many men were killed or wounded but nevertheless they succeeded in making an advance. It was 6th July before the Division was in the front line trenches ready for a further assault at 6a.m. the following day and there was heavy fighting in an attempt to take the village of Contalmaison. After two hours, and with much loss of life, they had succeeded, but unfortunately, after only two hours holding the village, they were driven back by a German counter offensive. The battle for the village raged for four days after which the British again took the village, this time managing to entrench on the side occupied by the Germans. Once again the Worcesters lost many men either killed or wounded, but so did the enemy, and the Division also took four thousand German prisoners. It was during this action that two men, Sam and Arthur Reynolds, were wounded – they had enlisted at the same time as Wilfrid and were from the same village.

Only 100 of the division had survived in the wet, with water and mud often up to their waist but they were soon in action again, this time, being outnumbered. They were almost out of ammunition and with their rifles often clogged up with mud, they were forced to retire five hundred yards over open ground and under heavy machine gun and artillery fire. Greatly to Wilfrid's sorrow, they were forced to leave their dead and wounded comrades behind. Their only drink during this five day period was from their water bottles which were filled on the first day and thereafter topped up with half a pint a day. Their only food consisted of what they had managed to capture from the Germans. Fighting continued until July 16th when relief soldiers took over. What was left of Wilfrid's Division then moved to Amiens station where, at 5.00p.m. they boarded a train for Béthune, arriving at 3a.m. the next day.

When he arrived in Béthune, Wilfrid was promoted to the rank of Corporal before being sent back to the bomb school where he trained to be an instructor. Following his time there, he re-joined his Battalion at Beuvry. The weather was very warm but the Section was kept busy digging trenches at La Bassie, which was in the brick fields. During the night, trench mortar and grenade fighting were very severe. Wilfrid's platoon was manning a mine crater only thirty yards from the Germans and he was kept busy at night with mine laying and repelling any German attack. He preferred to *be in a bayonet charge, as you go forward to be killed or to kill, and you think it is going to be the latter. In a heavy bombardment you can't do anything; you can't get your own back and you can't run away.'* In one of these enemy forays he killed a German soldier with his rifle whereas most of the time he was using grenades or bayonet. The crater which was his 'home' at this time had been created, a month earlier, by a German mine explosion in which eighty-six British soldiers were killed and buried. B Company's Sergeant Major and a number of Scottish soldiers were taken prisoner. After fighting day and night for most of July, they were finally relieved.

On August 2nd Wilfrid and his comrades were able to have some rest in a dugout in the village of Givenchy about five hundred yards behind the front line trenches. Three days later, The 'Ox and Bucks' (Oxfordshire and Buckinghamshire Regiment) took over the dugout and the Worcesters were able to march back to Béthune where they were billeted in a school. On the very next day, a Sunday, they attended a Church parade, which was held in the Grande Place. It was conducted by the chaplain in the presence of General Monroe, their Army Corps Commander, and three French Generals. The next day 15-inch, heavy calibre, German shells hit Béthune. They caused 20ft. deep craters that were 34ft. across. Unfortunately the hospital was hit and altogether 250 people were killed, including civilians and French and British military personnel.

August 8th saw the start of another spell of combat duty; this time in trenches at Hulluck just forward of Vermelles where the trenches were only twenty yards from the German lines. The fighting was very heavy with assault and counter assault from both sides but little ground changing hands. Sadly, one of the men, Private Brookes in Wilfrid's Section, was seriously wounded and later died at the Clearing Station. There was much loss of life on both sides with many bodies lying on the barbed wire. In another Company fifteen men and their Commanding Officer lost their lives. On August 13th one officer and three men died as a result of gas. It was not until 16th that Wilfrid was able to return to billets, this time at Sailly, about ten miles behind the front line.

The weather was very stormy in the latter half of September and this resulted in the trenches being very wet and muddy. Sometimes Wilfrid and his comrades were up to their waist in water and the chances for a bath were few and far between but very welcome when they came. The section and the platoon suffered heavy casualties at this time and he thought *'I wonder if my time is ever coming,'* He did not have to wait long.

Chapter Eleven

BLIGHTY 1

In the early hours of the morning on September 24th he was busily engaged in a bombing raid. He returned safely to the reserve trenches when a trench mortar exploded about 100 yards behind him; he watched the blast and then turned and walked down the trench. A piece of shrapnel (metal from the bomb case) buried itself in his back, but his only concern was *'should I get to Blighty!'* He was examined by a front-line doctor who told him that it was deeply embedded and he would have to return to England for it to be removed. He then went back to the nearest Dressing Station where his wound was dressed and he was inoculated. From there he went to the Clearing Station where he was marked for Base Hospital. He travelled by train to Boulogne, arriving at 10p.m. In the Field Hospital his wound was dressed and he had a bath, a good meal, and slept well. Early next morning he was wakened for breakfast followed by the doctor's round. The doctor marked some for Base Hospital and some for Blighty. *'However, I was lucky enough to get marked Blighty.'*

By 10a.m. on the morning of September 25th he was on the hospital ship bound for Southampton where he arrived at 1p.m. He caught a train to Manchester and from here he was transported two miles to the military hospital, arriving at 11p.m. The following day he was operated on to remove the deeply embedded shrapnel. The wound healed quickly and on October 9th he was transferred to the care of the Red Cross for post-operative convalescence. The Red Cross was housed in a school that had been converted to a recovery unit. Here, *'we had some jolly good times – concert parties etc.'* After only one month in England, on 25th of October, Wilfrid was certified fit and, after ten days home leave, joined the 5th Battalion Worcesters stationed at Tregantle Fort.

During the next six weeks he was busy instructing new recruits. Unlike his previous time at Tregantle he was now housed in a hut that had a small fireplace – quite a luxury as winter was approaching. They were allowed out of camp until 9.30p.m. each evening and could usually get army transport into town. Wilfrid was hoping that, after nineteen months in France, this more agreeable lifestyle would continue for some time, but it was not to be. After six weeks the order came for a draft of two hundred, mostly NCOs, to return to France. And so it was that after being medically graded A1 again, at 5a.m. on November 17th, they were marched to Devonport Station, band playing and crowds cheering them on. At Southampton they embarked on 'Mona's Queen' bound for France.

Chapter Twelve

BACK TO WAR

On arrival at Le Havre on December 18th it was snowing hard. During the night, while sleeping in tents *'packed in like sardines'*, there was a German bombing raid on the town. The next day they travelled by train to Rouen and from there they marched the six miles to the Base Camp. Here they were kept busy all day with gas tests, musketry training and bayonet practice. The only exception was on Sunday when they attended Church parade. On Christmas day they also attended Church parade. Unfortunately the food was *'about enough for a six years old child!'* Breakfast was one small loaf and a *'bit of ham'* between eight men who also had a pint of tea each. For lunch there was beef, potatoes, greens and a small portion of plum pudding. At teatime they were given *'bread and butter, as usual, and a plate of figs between eight men'*. On the last day of the year they marched back to Rouen and caught a train to Sailly on the southern Somme.

From Sailly a long march brought the contingent to where the 4th Battalion was billeted in Molliens-Vidame. On joining the 4th Battalion Wilfrid was confirmed *Paid Lance Sergeant*, and given a Platoon. The pay was 19 shillings and 10 pence per week. There was a great shortage of NCOs as many had lost their lives in battle. Here *'we joined our different Companies, mine being Z Company'*. After several days marching via various villages where they were sometimes billeted in houses, they finally arrived in the reserve trenches at Givenchy on January 17th. It was snowing. Taking two days rations of bully beef and biscuits the men marched to the front line trenches in front of Bapaume, where they found the town in ruins.

Ruins of Bapaume

January 1916 was a very cold month and as the trenches were often half filled with ice-cold water, many soldiers got frostbite. Life for the Company revolved around two days and nights in the trenches followed by two in the reserve trenches. Sometimes they were moved round various front line and reserve trenches. Sometimes they were allowed to march to various camps such as Givenchy, Mansell, Heilly or Carnay for one night's rest. This continued throughout most of February, the Company losing many men, both killed and wounded. Forward fighting between the Allied and German trenches was with rifle, bayonet and bomb. Mortar shells often landed in the trenches and larger shells with longer range devastated many miles behind the front line. There was also much aerial bombardment. On February 24th the 4th Battalion left their rest billets at La Houssaye and marched forward, relieving the 1st Essex Regiment in trenches facing Sailly, just north of St. Pierre Vast Wood. The next day a strong fighting patrol under Lieutenants B. Perkins and C.E. Hackett made a daring reconnaissance of the opposing line. The subsequent attack in the early hours of the 25th was the action in which Wilfrid sustained his most serious, life threatening injuries.

Chapter Thirteen

BLIGHTY 2

It was a night of bloody hand to hand fighting in no man's land. *'Guns were roaring, doing their work, bombs exploding and Very lights in the sky. The German Very lights were of different colours – white for illumination, red for reinforcements and green to call in the artillery.'* An exploding German bomb struck Wilfrid and although he survived, *'I lost nearly all my Platoon that night.'* He inhaled gas, had penetrating injuries to the head, neck and face, a fractured left arm, and most seriously of all, a smashed leg which had open wounds that were bleeding profusely. The leg was subsequently found to have five fractures. *'All I was looking for was a German to come and finish me off with the bayonet.'*

But that did not happen. After only a few minutes *'my own stretcher bearers came and dragged me away, catching hold of my legs and dragged me as it is impossible to get stretchers up so close when there is a battle in progress. They then tied my leg to a rifle to keep it together and bound my wounds up as well as possible.'* He was placed on the stretcher and the two men carried this fourteen-stone man three miles to the nearest forward dressing station (probably at Combles). There were many bomb craters on the way and they dropped him several times. It was a frosty night and *'I was nearly frozen to death, having my clothes cut off me to get at the wounds. I wished many times that I had died.'* The journey to the triage dressing station took several hours and once there his wounds were re-dressed and *'I must say the nurses were very brave.'* (Seeing such terrible injuries.)

On 27th February he was moved to a field hospital where, in addition to the open wounds in leg, back and head, he underwent surgery for his various wounds and fractures. He remained dangerously ill for ten days and was then moved by train to the General Hospital in Rouen. Unfortunately *'the journey was too much for me'* and he was operated on again, remaining dangerously ill for some time. He was very well treated in the hospital and was full of praise for the care he received. A month later he had improved and the doctor said that he was fit to travel to England. So it was that on April 14th he boarded the hospital ship *Western Australia*, leaving France for England, and for him the fighting was over.

Chapter Fourteen

BACK TO ENGLAND

After *'a painful journey'* he arrived at Southampton at 9a.m. on April 15th 1916. *'I was carried to the hospital train en route for Stockport, arriving at 9p.m.,'* and there he was to remain for almost two months. His stay was a time when his general health was being built up and the only treatment he received was the daily dressing of his wounds *'that were very painful.'* It was not until 10th June that he was well enough to be transferred to Knutsford in Cheshire.

While here, he underwent two further operations. He was well cared for and was as contented as possible under the circumstances. There were two 'red letter' days, the first being on July 20th when *'I was allowed to sit in a chair in my room for a few hours.'* The second occasion was a week later when *'I was able to go a little on crutches.'* Two days later there was a garden fete in Knutsford and the ambulant soldiers from the hospital were invited to attend. Wilfrid was determined to go. He was transferred by *'motor'* (car) and *'I was unlucky, for as I got out of the motor I fell down and re-fractured my leg, causing me to stay in bed for another three and a half months.'* The next day he was examined by a military doctor who ordered his transfer to Manchester Royal Infirmary *'and there I stayed until February 20th 1917'.*

When he returned to England, Wilfrid was disgusted to find that there were young men on strike for more pay and more food. *'Such men as those ought to be in the army comparing their money with the Tommy's few shillings a week. They can never realise there is a war on. Enough can never be done for the boys who have been risking their lives, some to sacrifice them.'* On hearing that the coal workers were on strike, the coal being essential for the munitions factories, he writes *'I could have shot the lot of them.'* On February 20th 1917 the doctor gave him his discharge papers and Wilfrid said to him, *'I have been waiting for them ever since 1914 and have only just found them!'* That ended his military career with an 80% disability.

Campaign and Victory Medals and Numbered Silver badge (awarded to those honourably discharged following injury)

POSTSCRIPT

When he arrived home by train, Wilfrid was met at the station by his parents. His head was still swathed in bandages and his left leg was strapped vertically to his body. (A mobility of hip he retained to the end of his life, becoming his 'party trick') and he was on crutches. His mother did not recognise him and remarked to her husband. *'I wonder who that poor fellow is.'* He continued to need dressings to leg, head and back and as a result of the head wound suffered from mild epileptic attacks but these soon disappeared. Back in Inkberrow, the District Nurse, Dorothy Howitt, tended his wounds and it was not long before they fell in love! He said they could not get married until he had a home for her and £1000 in the bank and it was 1926 before he achieved this.

It was obvious to him that, with one wasted, short, and completely stiff leg and a hole through the bone of his right temple, he would be unable to return to the family business. He decided to try market gardening and poultry farming, buying a patch of land in Worcestershire. Here he built a bungalow and set up his own wholesale business, growing and marketing produce that, together with his eggs, he supplied to shops in Stourbridge on a twice-weekly round.

As a young man he had been a fine cricketer and tennis player. The hand and eye co-ordination required for these sports is just what was required for a grenade thrower. On the land next to his bungalow he built a grass tennis court, taught himself to be ambidextrous with the racket and by this means, and by hopping, he regained something of his former skill. As far as cricket was concerned he liked nothing better than visiting the lovely Riverside County Ground in Worcester. Although he had no formal musical training he could play the piano 'by ear.' His favourite hymn was *Safe in the arms of Jesus* as he used to remark, *'you never knew whether the next day you would, indeed, be safe in the arms of Jesus.'* Ironically, on the day the Second World War was declared, the family was on holiday in Devonport with the Naval Commander (uncle Ritchie) who had befriended him during World War One.

This true account has been written not only as a tribute to my father but also as a tribute to all the other brave young men, many of whom lost their lives and whose heroism has not been recorded or recognised in this way.

The inscription reads:
Presented to Lance Sergt W. Barley
for Duty 1914-1918
From Inkberrow Friends

The pictures above were taken in 2010 showing the village that, in subsequent fighting, was later largely destroyed, but now restored. Also the area in front of Pierre Vast Wood where Wilfrid received his most severe injuries. In 1980 Wilfrid returned to the places, such as Bethune and Arras, that he had known in the Great War. His face, on seeing the war graves where many of his fellow soldiers are buried, showed that the mental scars inflicted by such a terrible war can never be erased.